Beautiful Lightning

Beautiful Lightning

Spiritual Poems in a Difficult World

Edward J. Rielly

RESOURCE *Publications* · Eugene, Oregon

BEAUTIFUL LIGHTNING
Spiritual Poems in a Difficult World

Resource Publications
An Imprint of Wipf and Stock Publishers
199 W. 8th Ave., Suite 3
Eugene, OR 97401

www.wipfandstock.com

PAPERBACK ISBN: 978-1-5326-8063-2
HARDCOVER ISBN: 978-1-5326-8064-9
EBOOK ISBN: 978-1-5326-8065-6

Manufactured in the U.S.A.

For my parents, who modeled a spiritual life; and for my wife, Jeanne, who has guided by example

Contents

Acknowledgments

Many of the poems in this collection, sometimes in slightly different form, have appeared in the following magazines and anthologies:

Ancient Paths: "One Father to Another"

Aurorean: "A Quiet Warning"

Avocet: "My Seasons"

Caveat Lector: "Morning," "Sons and Fathers"

Cloudbank: "The Priest was Wrong about Shepherds"

Delta Epsilon Sigma Journal: "A Child's Death," "Beautiful Lightning," "Communion Gathering," "Divine Theories," "Genesis," "God's Grace," "Mirror Images," "Racing to the Tomb," "Revealing the Mystery," "Seven Signs," "The Host," "The Natural Order," "Three Shadows," "To G.M. Hopkins"

Kennebec: A Portfolio of Maine Writing: "Delacroix's Blood"

Kind of a Hurricane Press: Anthology: Switch (The Difference): "Large Brown Eyes"

Mobius: "Buddy"

Poetry Explosion Newsletter: "Tiger Lilies"

Potpourri: "For a Poet whose Strength Failed Him"

Promise Magazine: "'By Faith, not by Sight,' It reads," "From Almost Nothing"

Shemom: "Food Pantry"

Time of Singing: "Barsabbas," "Our Journey to Emmaus"

Waterways: "Ourselves," "Silent Pointing"

WestWard Quarterly: "The Candle"

Wolf Moon Journal: "Small Pieces of Her Life," "Time"

Words and Images: "The Waking of the Trees"

Beautiful Lightning

What does He ask of us?
Death on the cross,
lingering pain, aching
immeasurable in our souls?

Or joy, feeling the beauty in
small things, the baby's crawl,
an old woman's eyes seeking
her past in faces around
a breakfast table,
the soft thrust of a hand
into a sheep's thick wool?

The new lamb cavorts,
leaps onto its mother's back;
left alone in the pen
it bleats its sorrow from deep down
in its simple lamb soul.

When the rains come and summer
storms rip the sky, the tree
the sheep huddle under is both
threat and salvation. Yet even
the lightning is beautiful.

Communion Gathering

It is Sunday morning and
they are lined up for communion
at Dunkin' Donuts, each car
caressing the vehicle in front,
the one behind, unbroken chain
of celebrants in their early
morning sacred liturgy.

How strong the dark black wine
pumping life into veins,
surging presence of the bright
morning of the remainder
of their lives, awake now, shaking
heads in time to music
playing softly on auto radios.

It is the host, though, that most
attracts, magnetic pull reaching
into highways, into well-kept
split-level homes, drawing multitudes
more forcefully than loaves and fish,
sweet chocolate filling, jelly donut,
cruel crullers in their ridged sugar,
white cream rolling over tongues.

The spirit unites through nerve
endings crying sweetness, fulfillment,
the long line snaking slowly toward
a faceless voice out of somewhere,
out of a succulent Sunday somewhere,
asking for four dollars, thirty cents.

Revealing the Mystery

The mortal coil unwinds for all:
        the aged
        the ill
        those dwelling,
        however youthful
        and vibrant,
        on the cliff's edge,

those who recognize the slow
        or sudden
approach, the stranger
        at the door,

who see the flame rise,
        sink,
and in the interim
recognize, at the center
        of their being,
        a great mystery:
        Who is,
        Who will be.

The Natural Order

Introduction:

The plagues of Exodus, as many biblical scholars have pointed out, are based on natural phenomena transformed, in the biblical account, into supernatural events to demonstrate God's superiority to the Egyptian deities. In the following haiku, I return to natural realities in their often benign, even sometimes beautiful, manifestations.

1

from the dock
child's arm stretching
toward a red stone

2

frog retreats
from a flower bed . . .
one less green leaf

3

weeding flowers –
gnats cause me to pull
a marigold by mistake

4

under a sheltering
elm I share my snack
with a fly or two

5

dry river bed –
old man gently lifts
the dead lamb

6

mosquito bite
stinging the arm
I place around you

7

after the storm
girl gathering hailstones
before they can melt

8

a grasshopper
interrupts my view
of the tiger lily

9

evening darkness –
I reach out to touch
the cool air

10

wind rustling
a bedroom curtain . . .
our baby bats his mobile

Seven Signs

heavy baptismal font –
baby's cries rise
from the water

through a dark screen
the priest's soft words . . .
somewhere a car braking

First Communion Mass –
in her pew a girl practicing
the Sign of the Cross

taking a new name
the boy with pimples now
a soldier for Christ

bride's white glove
on her father's arm . . .
a child's scraped knee

on the old stone steps
red rose pinned to her dress
she calls her son father

last anointing –
afterward the woman
listening to rain

All One

Sunshine can be
      a cloudy day,
      a day full of rain
pelting the windows,

a day of pure white
      on blue,
a slow breeze barely
affirming existence
      of air,

a purple cloud trudging
      over sky
      carrying its weight
      like stones,

or a bright, blazing blast
      of lightness
      blinding eyes so one sees
      in the brightness
      only by turning away,

or even the darkness behind
      shut eyes:
it is all one,
      all God's presence.

The Priest Was Wrong About Shepherds

The priest explained,
in his homily, sun slanting
over his left shoulder, that in real
life a shepherd would never leave
his ninety-nine sheep for one,
no matter how prized,
that it made no economic sense
to do that, not then, in Jesus' time,
not now. He was quite certain.

Yet I know how important that one
truly would be, not metaphorically, not
as the subject of a parable (to be fair
I must state that the priest valued highly
the lost sinner, just not the wandering sheep),
but as a real, flesh and blood, bleating,
lost sheep, its white wool dirty, bedraggled
from its lonely exodus, its forlorn status
as the missing sheep. Yes, I know about
sheep, and the priest was wrong.

Once upon a time far back in my youth
I raised sheep, seeing them not as subjects
for parables or homilies but as work
and money, a child's, then teenager's
part-time job on my parents' farm.
Friends pumped gas, clerked in stores,
while I raised sheep, selling their wool
in large round bundles sheared
and tied methodically, firmly, by our
hired sheep shearer, a man of
unparalleled skill in removing a fleece
in one multifaceted whole, almost,
if I were into parables, like Jesus'
seamless garment for which Romans
cast dice rather than tear asunder.

But the sheep were more than that
for me: friends, pets, companions.
I fed them, named them, ensured that
abundant water waited in their troughs.
And when one ewe brought forth twins
and then died, I raised those orphans,
feeding them in old 7-Up bottles filled
with cow's milk and Karo syrup,
watched them tugging at the rubber
nipples I attached to the bottles,
watched their tails swinging furiously
as they inhaled that milk. I named them
Katie and Sam after an aunt and uncle,
and although Sam did not have a long life
I could call Katie for years after
and she, then aging, would still hurry
to me. And when she broke a leg
trying to stretch on her hind legs
after leaves hanging from a tree
I took her, lying in the box of our
old Ford pick-up, to town, where
the veterinarian, not once smirking
at my determination to heal her
broken leg, attached a splint and
sent us on our way with his best wishes.

So, you see, the priest was wrong.
Yes, I was not quite a shepherd,
and I did not have to worry about
my remaining sheep ripping through
a fence to wander away in my absence.
Yet I cannot believe that a shepherd,
even in Jesus' time, would not seek
after even one missing sheep. That is not
the way of people who care about sheep.

Ourselves

We recognize ourselves in
the faces that we see.
The faces that look nothing
like ours when we gaze into
a bathroom mirror, study old
photographs entombed in plush-
covered albums. Different noses,
hair of other colors, a mole
not present in the person staring
at us in the park, on a street.

Yet there we are: something
in the glint of an eye, the jaw's
jauntiness, the way lips purse.
We cannot quite figure it out,
this strangely unfamiliar,
familiar connection, but we
are there. Perhaps it is the soul
or a dream working its way
out, or a fear we share.
Perhaps, for just a moment
in their own silence, they also
see us –and themselves –
and that is why they do not
turn away at once, instead
loiter, allow a few seconds
to pass, then shift aside,
leaving us once again to search,
alone or in a crowd, for ourselves.

Silent Pointing

At the doctor's office, a little girl
who cannot seem to speak points
above the ledge behind which
the receptionist sits, points above
the receptionist's head.

Her mother follows the girl's index finger
for just a moment, then returns to
her insurance form, her pen moving
slowly from blank to blank while
her daughter pulls her hand back
to her side, silently watching
whatever she saw in her quiet life,
something neither her busy mother
nor my questioning gaze can see.
She stands immobile, locked into
a vision no one else can share.

Barsabbas

(Acts 1:23–26)

What did you think, Barsabbas,
when you were turned aside, rejected,
after serving loyally during your master's
dangerous ministry, in favor of Matthias,
marking you as unworthy
of being one of the select twelve,
a person assigned to anonymity,
a name recorded only once, then forgotten
forever by later generations?

What did you do then? Were you the loyal
soldier, obeying, struggling forward to die
along some dusty road in a strange land,
still trying to preach, you with so little voice?
Or did disappointment, shame at missing out
on your chance for fame,
drive you to despair, to apostasy even,
perhaps drinking yourself to death on cheap
wine in a harlot's false, comforting arms?

Let us think the former, that you, despite
your so brief appearance in the chronicle
of that great messianic movement, kept
the faith, retained the dedication that
sustained you in the shadow of the three
somber trees on the hillside. So, almost
nameless, taken for granted, worthy only of
a disappointing shadow, a brief drop of rain
quickly evaporating, we, too, may rise,
invisibly, unremembered, a name echoing like
a memory forgotten yet lurking in some
far corner of the collective mind, rising
to that place where all are remembered,
all are chosen, one way or another.

My Seasons

The warm, wet mud I dig in the vegetable
garden, the comforting aroma of alfalfa
just mown, fall leaves shaping my own
brown study in the back yard, snow hanging
like soft woolen blankets from pine branches,
and the steady, unending repetition that,
more than prayer, promises always tomorrow.

Out of Chaos

Before my eyes saw,
there was nothing. Slowly,
a murky membrane hinted
at order, meaning, beyond
itself. Sunshine was absent,
darkness grew only gradually
less dark, and voices
somewhere seemed to call.
Then the mist began to clear,
shapes intervened to pull
vision out of chaos. Sizes
materialized, colors woke senses,
the vague became definite,
the uncertain, certain,
the insecure, fixed.
My eyes saw what seemed,
then saw what was.
All came to fit, each piece
in its place, all registering
through deepening eyes
that see, order, and confirm.

Always Day

We close nighttime,
put it away in a drawer.
It is all daytime between us
even when we taste sorrow,
feel the weight of years,
hear echoes we cannot
understand even when
we are quiet and listen.
It is still day, sun shining
in your hair,
warmth touching me,
a breeze carrying what
we only sometimes understand
but always feel,
like a leaf touching skin.

Food Pantry

stocking shelves
I place each item
label outward,
neatness as pervasive
as at any supermarket

a few volunteers
and so many clients
sharing a space
constructed around food,
around need and dignity

at the check-in desk
a man offers no
proof of residency,
under the bridge having
no discernible address

at closing time
a handful of onions,
some apples softened:
leftovers, like all of us,
from a world of plenty

Buddy

We called him Buddy, everyone did,
that cousin who bribed me into
my first haircut with a peppermint
stick, and whose name fit his ready
enlistment as everybody's friend.

Above all, he loved to talk, mixing
stories, often not entirely true, with
a ready smile and quick laughter. Work
could wait, even if the cows got milked
an hour late, or rain came down before

the hay got safely tucked away, baled
and dry. There was always another
time to work. We wondered how he made
ends meet, but he did, and the stories
flowed like water from a faucet.

When I saw him last he no longer knew
me or the stories he had told before.
Are you related to me? he asked my
sister. I just came in from the field,
he said, there in the hallway of a

small-town nursing home. What tricks
nature plays on minds, I thought.
Yet as we sat in the lobby and
talked about things he no longer
remembered, there was still the smile,

the laughter, the same nod of head,
the same intonation. A young girl entered
and he asked her what grade she was in.
He did not know her any more than he
knew us that day, but he was still

clearly Buddy, and we sat and talked
of things his memory had lost, at least
a little consoled by what remained.

The Day His Cousin Died

They came in droves after
his cousin died, the man who
had paved his way, called
him forth, anointed him the one.

His cousin had been a simple man,
living in caves, eating honey and,
when hunger gnawed at his insides,
locusts he cooked over a small
fire. He owned nothing,
gave it all up for his young
cousin. No complaints.

The older man's virtue was well
known, widely respected, an affront
to those who found sin savory
as a bowl of sweet red wine.
Chastised for lusting after his
sister-in-law, Herod the tetrarch
threw him into prison, then
vacillated, longing to kill him
but afraid of stirring up trouble,
inciting the man's followers.

Then a sensuous dance by the daughter
of Herod's mistress led that sex-
crazed king to his fatal promise.
He served up the man's head
on a platter, the woman working
through her daughter for revenge
on the man who tried to spoil a good
thing she had going. A sad death, indeed.

So the young cousin went off by
himself to mourn, wanting to be
alone. Yet those who loved him
and his cousin knew that sorrow
needs company, and they came,
following the young man, opening
their hearts to him. He could
not send them away, not then.

The day rolled on and the crowd
mourned with the young man,
women weeping for the dead one,
their children only feebly
understanding. The men in attendance
tried to remain calm in their
grief, to set an example.

Then the time for eating came and
went, hunger spreading among
the crowd, children asking for food.
When the young man saw this, he instructed
his disciples to gather fish and
loaves, and he blessed them, the food
coming out of baskets that seemed
bottomless. All ate, the young man
giving to those who shared his
grief, the miracle coming down through
the ages, but everyone forgetting
that it was about grief rather
than mysterious multiplying, about
two beloved cousins, one dying then,
one living on to join his cousin
a few short years later, fulfilling
all sorts of difficult prophecies.

God's Grace

Raining slowly,
imperceptibly,
drop by slow drop,
my shirt dry for decades
until the first faint
touch of dampness,
a minute spot,
making itself known,
the rain working its way through,
drop piling on drop,
finally touching,
only now,
my skin,
the cool,
refreshing rain
working itself through
until, at last,
I feel something unmistakably
cool and wet.

The Host

The white disk circles
within itself, contracting
more forcefully than
the powerful inversion
of space-matter into
a black hole, its pull
stronger, its bulk cosmic,
its reach timeless,
a small piece of bread
pulling us inward,
feeding the world.

Divine Theories

If God can be figured
geometrically as a triangle,
why not as a circle
for eternity, a cube for
perfect symmetry?
Or a string to modernize
the theory, marking space
for all time? Or, containing
everything, a black dot,
the universe enclosed?

A Child's Death

Sorrow drags pieces from the heart,
anguish scratches the skies,
mothers and fathers grope
after meaning, their hands
empty, cribs and rooms
wilting in their emptiness.

Only the passing heart knows
the value of a gentle hand
welcoming at the moment of death,
the softly spoken word
to ease passage from hurt,
to dissolve terror into the waiting
shadow of light called God.

Mirror Images

Morning comes dovetailing
out of darkness, fanning
its great tail back and forth
trying to right the twist
and turn of uncertainty,
conjuring the spirit of
future, spreading dreams.
I prepare for what comes,
carefully sorting out my
works and days, measuring
the present in minutes,
seeing what will be, what
approaches, in my mirror.

In the mirror I see more
than I want. It is always
there, immeasurable, past
and present, uncertain by
fits and starts whether
the two measure up to future.
Gradually the hours lead
into darkness no matter how
hard I try. The coolness
of twilight, the chill of
dark, uncertainty felt deep
inside the bones, waiting
until the morning comes.

Genesis

and so God took chaos,
kissed its head,
patted its bottom,
and sent it off into daytime
to blossom in a thousand colors

and so Adam courted Eve
with a rib, and she
never complained,
loving all those flowers
in that gorgeous garden

and so the family
was penned in with animals
mooing and snorting,
air reeking with animal smells
and everybody seasick

and so it was hard
tiptoeing across the river
without getting feet wet,
their mother screaming,
"you get wet, I'll kill you!"

and so they trekked
for decades through dust, up and
down mountains, sun beating
on heads, and not a good walking
shoe among the lot of them

The Candle

The wax of many colors,
dripping, slides down
slowly, collects
in vertical ridges,
like veins, along the way.
Brittle shards break,
melt into one another.
The candle shortens
but its substance,
transformed, remains,
the colors mingling
in new ways, hues we
have never seen before.
From its glow the world
awakens, eyes
see, a hand reaches
as it has for countless
years. How beautiful
is this world still
in the candle's
quiet glimmering.

My Young Brother

I have waited all these years,
my brother, to see you, the infant
my parents lost so early, first born
to our family. I never knew you,

of course, born almost twenty years
after your brief life, not even
a picture of you, a fact my young
granddaughter, striking to the core

of sorrow, labeled "so sad." You lived
one month eighty-five years ago, dying
one year to the day before a second son
was born. It must have been a date

with some consolation for our mother,
although having never lost a child,
I can barely imagine her pain, my father's
mourning, the great emptiness such

a small object, an infant, can create.
How will you appear when I see you?
Will you be an infant still, an old man
reaching out a hand to another old man,

or someone in the prime of life?
We wait, unknowing, hoping that faith
has not been misplaced, our expectation
that coming home is always a family affair.

"By Faith, Not By Sight," It Reads

The quiet afternoon yields
to the ocean's roar,
crashing of waves

against boulders;
thunder grinds the sky
and the temperature drops

until I retreat to
the shelter of tall pines
out of the wind.

A young woman jogs by wearing
a white T-shirt that reads
"We walk by faith,

not by sight." As mist closes
over the offshore islands
lightning snakes through

the darkening sky,
the jagged flames
and rising wind

Elijah's chariot.
When I look again
the woman is gone.

The Waking of the Trees

In the back yard the young locust has begun
to bud, its short branches barely showing green.
An assortment of bushes planted over our two decades
of living here, of bringing life to our ground,
join the ceremony: the spirea, the burning bush,
still far from its bright, shocking red,
forsythias (the most numerous of our plantings) birthed
from branches taken from other branches.

The pine trees have never lost their green, though
it is good to see they have not browned in a winter's
blight, and the other trees, the weeping willow
that has grown so much, shooting its roots toward
our water lines, that we almost wish we had never dug it
into our lives. And the plum tree that each fall drops
buckets of small, hard plums before they ripen.
These too are turning green. And the birds in their
singing seem to rejoice with us.

But this year we notice the slowness of the poplars,
three tall trees in a line dividing our ground
from our neighbor's. They seem to balk at greening,
the slowness troubling us, for we have not yet
faced the death of trees in our back yard.

They stand as still as death, the branches close
against their trunks as if holding in against the wind,
the brown so brittle, though, they look too ready
to yield together to a sudden storm. The three
of them have died as one, we finally conclude.
No settling gradually into illness, leaves discolored,
twigs falling, scraping and groaning against fall,
no sickening thuds within a winter snowstorm.
They have left us without warning, all together,

as if some fate had decreed their death
a joint exercise, or a collective atonement for what
we may have done, or not done, through the years.
I lay my ax and saw sadly on the ground, and touch
the roughness of their silent trunks, before I cut.

One Father to Another

We pass on this fatherness
through the sky of centuries,
the blueness sparkling with sunlight,
white clouds lifting generation
after generation to eternity.
The father in me looks backward

as to the present. There are images
more real than any concrete shape
positioning itself before my eyes –
an old man leaning beside a radio,
the whisper of oxygen pledging life
with quiet lies, the fields
he harvested now green, golden.
Once again the rich black earth
turns over, soft and moist, crumbling
in a child's soft, grasping hand.

We fathers recede into photographs,
then pass beyond the camera –beyond
the stark figure with heavy
moustache, a woman in frills and lace
at his side, the man seated before
a farmhouse in the middle of young men
and women looking only faintly
like people I should remember –

until there are no photographs,
no images frozen in consciousness
or in the dark recesses of moments
between awake and sleep, until only
names on paper call out "father!"
and then only the emptiness of thought.

You are so young to be a father,
alive in all the living colors
of the day. Like the single yellow rose
your mother brings me, you are
the stalk and petals of my day.

Our Journey to Emmaus

My wife rides in the car
with me. It is old, rusted,
shaky. Its tires threaten to deflate.
The handle on the driver's door tilts,
threatens to come loose, held by
a bent screw. Rain seeps in
through a door always slightly ajar.

Sometimes I drive; sometimes she does.
We feel the gravel spitting under tires,
wind from passing trucks shaking us.
The transmission catches at crucial moments:
climbing a hill, passing a slow-moving
SUV, a child through the window frowning
at us. Our brakes squeal as a squirrel
starts, stops, darts across the road.

We are almost at our destination.
The journey has been long, and we are
hungry, thirsty, yet we are almost there.
Each mile we have traveled on
this long drive, from inside our car
seems, despite it all, to be a trip
we would have made no other way.

Morning

I seldom think of my mother and father
sleeping side by side, hands crossed,
fingers frozen around eternal rosaries.

Instead, Father calls the cows from
the back pasture, his voice waking morning,
and the cows answer in their steady walk

up the path marked by hoof-worn dirt
and cattle droppings, the slow, steady
progression to the cows' sacrifice.

Mother tends the stove and turns water
into coffee, the givings of soil into
hot, white cereal and brown toast.

It is morning, and all things are risen.
The rooster has crowed more than three times,
stanchions rattle in a foggy distance,

cold rises from a stove that knows no fuel,
and the son grows older than his father.

From Almost Nothing

A child comes from nothing,
or almost nothing –a puff
of air, a twitch of love spreading
like rain puddles, a dream
of things lasting forever.

When it is all over –the bulging
abdomen, the morning sickness,
the rush to the hospital, the uncertain
waiting, the woman's pain,
the man's emptiness –the named
and renamed thing called child
ties with bonds indissoluble,
compresses the world in a small fist.

Time

Photograph after photograph
we age slowly, suddenly
retreat to childhood when you
were neither anticipated nor realized
in my life. In your earliest
moments, I did not exist.

Our photographs fill book after book
that piled one above another
could reach the ceiling.
Together, as we read our lives,
we reach slowly toward
what we have become.

Against our window the rain
washes away illusion. The wind
that rises sings a voiceless song,
a melody to the years.
At night, in the stars,
we see each other again
as we were, as we will be.

Tiger Lilies

Number thirty-four, an anniversary
well after one milestone, just before
another, yet important. This year we make
a pilgrimage to origins, the houses
we inhabited in our youth, before we knew
that we would come together, hold each other,
like one of your magnets on the refrigerator.

We plant more flowers this summer,
color covering our yard and deck.
Each way we turn brightness almost
blinds us, a warm caravansary of annuals,
like children always young. Against the back
wall of our house, though, the tiger lilies
grow tall again and open their reddish-
orange, curling petals as they have done
so often. They remind me, especially,
of you, the color of your hair when we
first met, the message to me as silent
and as certain as the small notes
you secreted in my luggage on my
return to parents that first year of ours.
Tonight again we lie together, age
circling comfortably around our bed.
No fear touches me when you are near.
The flowers bloom warmly outside our window.

Small Pieces of Her Life

She broke the bread into
small pieces, like the fragments
of her life spread out in layers
of rearing children, raising
chickens and turkeys for extra
money for those things not essential,
like children's toys, a Sunday
dress. Carefully she worked
the dry half-loaf into pieces,
mixed in two eggs just gathered
from the hen house. Without measuring
she measured in a quarter cup of sugar,
twice as much of sweet dark raisins,
two tablespoons of oleo, cheaper
than butter, but something she did
not talk about with other dairy
wives, and a cup of the milk my father
brought each morning, warm and frothy,
from the cow barn. In her old pan,
lightly greased with lard,
the pudding baked for three-fourths
an hour, a time she watched carefully
on a grease-speckled clock
on the wall above the oven.

While the aroma of the baking
pudding spread invitingly from
room to room, she prepared the
topping that made her bread pudding
a delicacy I can still taste five
decades later, still imitate
in my modern kitchen so imperfectly.

It was all sweetness: a cup of sugar,
one and a half teaspoons of cinnamon,
oleo (a teaspoon this time), held together
with three tablespoons of flour,
measurements again she knew by sight,
which years later she put down on
paper for a son whose sight was so
much different. She then would add
a cup and half of cold water and mix,
stirring the ingredients cautiously
on a black, gas-lit burner, not
letting the topping burn, keeping
the sweetness turning, until her
spoon felt firm resistance, and all
that remained would be to pour
the heavy, thick, sweet substance
over the raisin-filled pudding
and watch the rest of us making our
spoons move quickly, surely.

Delacroix's Blood

Large drops of blood, bright and wet,
two horses shying from the scene, a hand
both pointing and pulling back, perhaps
frightened by some overwhelming truth.
But above all the blood on the body hanging
on the cross.

A self-portrait, I imagine, this painting
of the Crucifixion. The painter feeling blood
in his veins bursting forth, the lance stirring
in himself, point searching his short life.

The horses know. They sense the awful
moment that has fallen. They pull, and,
off-canvas, snort and buck against
their riders. Their strong bodies feel
the frailty of muscle and of bone.

That hand bothers me. How at the moment
of identification, as in saying "That man
is dead!" the consequence hits home.
It pulls back. Yes, I cannot see it withdrawing,
but I know. It is impossible to miss
that horror, and my hand clenches where it hangs.

The painter's hand paints with power strokes,
his brush alive and sweeping. It is all motion
and might. But he knows. The blood betrays
his secret. He knows what dies eventually.

For a Poet Whose Strength Failed Him

After years of putting
muscle to words, cramming
strength into vision,
roaming fields of nuance,
wrestling meaning
into small moments
that took flight like
lightning, blasting truths,
often unpleasant but
important nonetheless,
into the sky of our sight,

you found a leg giving
way, an arm dropping
its cradle of books,
your youngest child
too heavy for hoisting
onto a summer branch,

and then, finally,
some three years later,
finger by finger
placing words, slowly,
onto a small screen,

until you no longer
could lift a finger
to help your vision
of this world
take shape,

and all the power
and truth
of your poetry
contracted
to one small
point of light
driving inward
to the center
of your being
and imploding
like a great
star crashing
into itself,
into the vision
we all seek.

To G. M. Hopkins

Your golden age, your shook-foil world
over, if worlds can end when God shines
forth in every nook and cranny of your being –
I count my years and equal yours.
The rod you kissed scrapes hard
against my lips, the bone-hold of the awful hand
stretches muscles, joints out of place,
and sometimes the grave seems more certain
than your, ah! bright heaven.

Sons and Fathers

You cried without, I think, knowing why
until a cousin whose name I couldn't
remember, and still can't, lifted you
out of my arms, from my father's house

of death, to walk you back and forth
on the shaded sidewalk where tall, graceful
elms held out the blistering August sun.
When she returned, you were asleep.

Inside, we sat on gray folding chairs
to stare at death's image, grasped hands
of condolence, answered mumbles
and halting, half-embarrassed clichés,

frail boats in which friends paddled
against their own knowledge
of mortality. Staring at the thin cold
fingers interlocked around a rosary,

I felt with new certainty the mortal union
of the father in the coffin, the son sitting
straight backed on a hard iron chair, and you
asleep in the arms of that nameless cousin.

Three Shadows

The three Wise Men cast
shadows on the snow.
I see only the shadows but
I know they are here,
the journey long from where
they found an infant squealing
for food, his mother rocking him
in her thin young arms,
the time not yet ripe for feeding,
years yet from her loss.

Here to Maine they have carried
their secrets, their knowledge of
mystery, of what the future promises,
of life and death, of sacrifice
we all must make, willing
or not. The shadows turn red
in the sunset. Somewhere outside
a baby cries, the sound rising
like smoke in the cold winter air.

Hospice

The closed eyes open
but do not follow as
I move from head
to foot of the bed
and back again.

They stare as if the object
of sight, if sight there be,
is somewhere through me,
through walls and doors,
beyond wood and concrete;

or perhaps within the slowly
disintegrating life that lies
quietly, barely breathing,
tucked into the brain
of the patient, into the person
we, around her bed, love.

Racing to the Tomb

Peter and John race to the tomb,
the body missing, they were told,
the young man, athletic, agile,
outdistancing his companion. Peter,
puffing his way across the hard,
rocky surface, his sandals stirring
a thin layer of dust.

The young man arrives first,
waits, catching his breath, defers
to Peter, only a little from fear,
wanting to know, yet not wanting
the knowledge that will forever define
his life. So he waits, while Peter,
his chest heaving, arrives at the opening,
the entrance into the dark cavity
of death, of emptiness, of hope.

A Quiet Warning

Autumn creeps forward, cold filters
through nights, touching lightly
the geraniums still blooming in red,
hanging baskets of multi-colored petunias,
marigolds stretching over their pots
like tiny suns just rising or setting.
Cold leaves a quiet warning,
an occasional flower wizened in falling
temperatures, leaves starting to drop
from stems still green. It is a warning
that flowers and I must heed.
It is a sign that things end, no matter
their beauty, or their constant efforts
to brighten even the darkest of days.
But, I remember, there is also spring.

Large Brown Eyes

Daisies wink with large
brown eyes. It is
the summer wink, lilacs
gone but flowers enough yet
to people a garden.

A woman strolls by
pushing a carriage,
the little girl swinging
her arms like flowers
swaying in the breeze.

Large golden marigolds
as big as a man's fist
bob gently, and purple
petunias billow out
around their hanging pot.

When night falls
the child reaches for her
favorite stuffed animal,
the heliotropes, darker even
than petunias, recede

first into darkness, followed,
finally, by even the dazzling
marigolds –each night a winter,
each morning another spring giving
way to another shining summer.

www.ingramcontent.com/pod-product-compliance
Lightning Source LLC
Chambersburg PA
CBHW060431050426
42449CB00009B/2240